Let's Match the Animals

GOOD JOB!

Sticker

Point to the animal that matches the one in the example.

Let's Match the Clothes

To Parents: Guide your child by pointing to the hat and saying, "Look at the colors and shape of the hat. Then, find another hat that looks the same." Repeat the process with the shorts.

GOOD JOB!

Sticker

Point to the object that matches the one in the example.

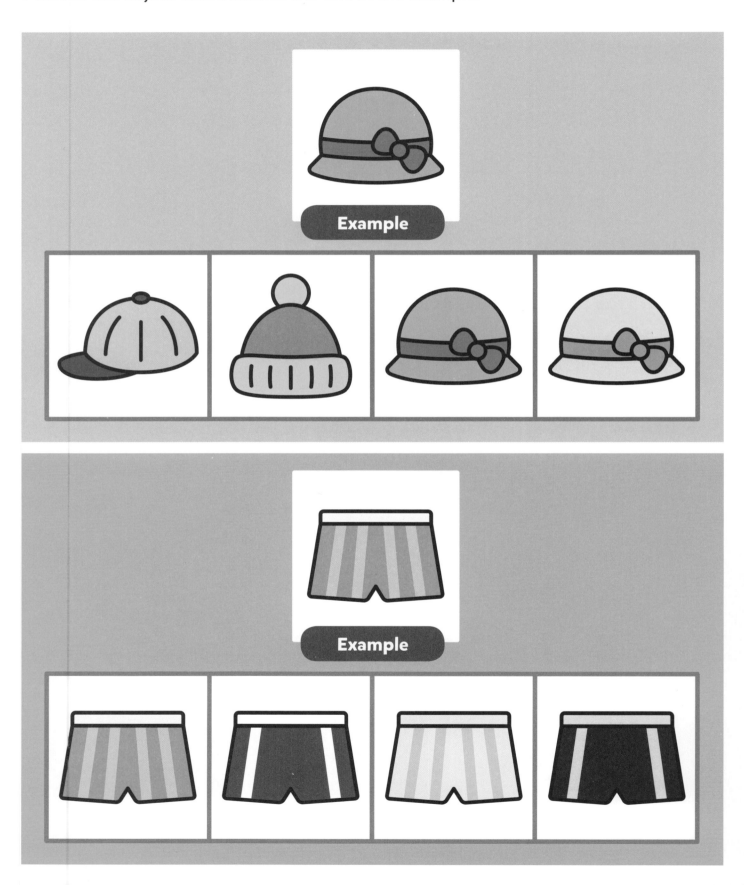

Example

Example

Let's Match the Trucks

To Parents: Begin by pointing to each utility truck in the example box and asking, "What kind of truck is this?" Say the name of each truck, and then have your child identify its match.

GOOD JOB!

Sticker

Which truck matches each truck in the example box?
Point with your finger.

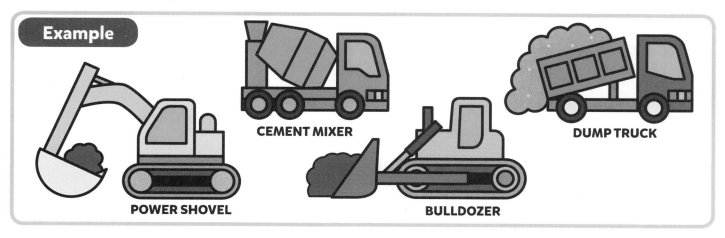

Example

CEMENT MIXER

DUMP TRUCK

POWER SHOVEL

BULLDOZER

4

Let's Match the Vehicles

To Parents: Point to each vehicle in the example box and ask "What kind of vehicle is this?" Say the name of each vehicle, and then have your child identify its match.

3

GOOD JOB!
Sticker

Which vehicle matches each vehicle in the example box?
Point with your finger.

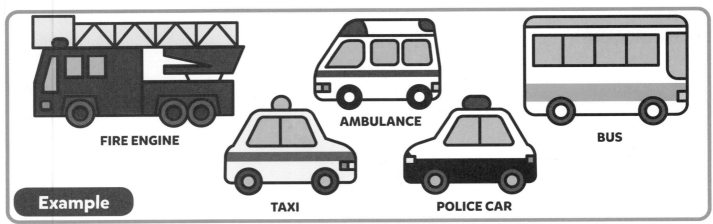

FIRE ENGINE

AMBULANCE

BUS

TAXI

POLICE CAR

Example

Let's Count

To Parents: Discuss with your child that there is one hippo and one strawberry sticker. Then, ask your child to place the strawberry sticker inside the hippo's mouth.

GOOD JOB!
Sticker

Put 1 sticker inside the 1 hippo's mouth.

Sticker

Let's Count

To Parents: Have your child point to and count the two animals, the two forks, and the two plates. Make sure that he or she understands that there are two of each object. Then, do the activity.

GOOD JOB!
Sticker

Put 1  sticker on each of the 2 animals' plates.

Sticker

Sticker

Let's Count

To Parents: Have your child point to and count the three hamsters. Then, using the stickers from the front of the book, ask your child to put one seed sticker between each hamster's hands.

Put 1 sticker in each of the 3 hamsters' hands.

Let's Draw Straight Lines

To Parents: Have your child use a thick crayon or marker to draw a line from the dog to the bone. It is okay if your child goes outside of the white area. He or she will get better with practice.

Draw lines that connect the dogs with the bones.

Let's Draw Curves

To Parents: Have your child use a thick crayon or marker to draw the curved lines below. Make the activity more fun by creating monkey and squirrel sounds as the animal moves down the tree.

Draw lines that connect Monkey to his banana and Squirrel to her acorn.

Let's Draw Curves

To Parents: Have your child use a thick crayon or marker to draw the curved lines below. Help make the activity fun by creating swimming sounds (*splash, splash*).

Draw lines that connect the children to the fish.

Let's Draw with a Square

To Parents: Encourage your child to draw an original face and not just copy one of the examples. After your child is finished, ask, "What did you draw?" Say, "It looks wonderful."

Draw a face using a ☐.

Example

Let's Draw with a Circle

To Parents: Encourage your child to draw an original face and not just copy the examples. After your child is finished, ask, "What kind of face did you draw?" Praise specific features of the drawing.

Draw a face using a ◯.

Example

Let's Use Animal Stickers

To Parents: Use the giraffe, lion, zebra, elephant, and rhinoceros stickers from the front of the book. After your child places the animal stickers, ask, "What kinds of animals do you see?"

Put animal stickers in the picture.

Let's Use Insect Stickers

To Parents: Use the stickers from the front of the book. After your child places the animal stickers, ask, "What kinds of insects do you see?" This activity builds fine motor skills.

Put insect stickers anywhere in the picture.

Let's Use the Merry-Go-Round Sticker

To Parents: After your child has placed the merry-go-round sticker, pretend to go to the amusement park together. Pretend to ride all the different rides with your child.

Put the merry-go-round sticker anywhere in the picture.

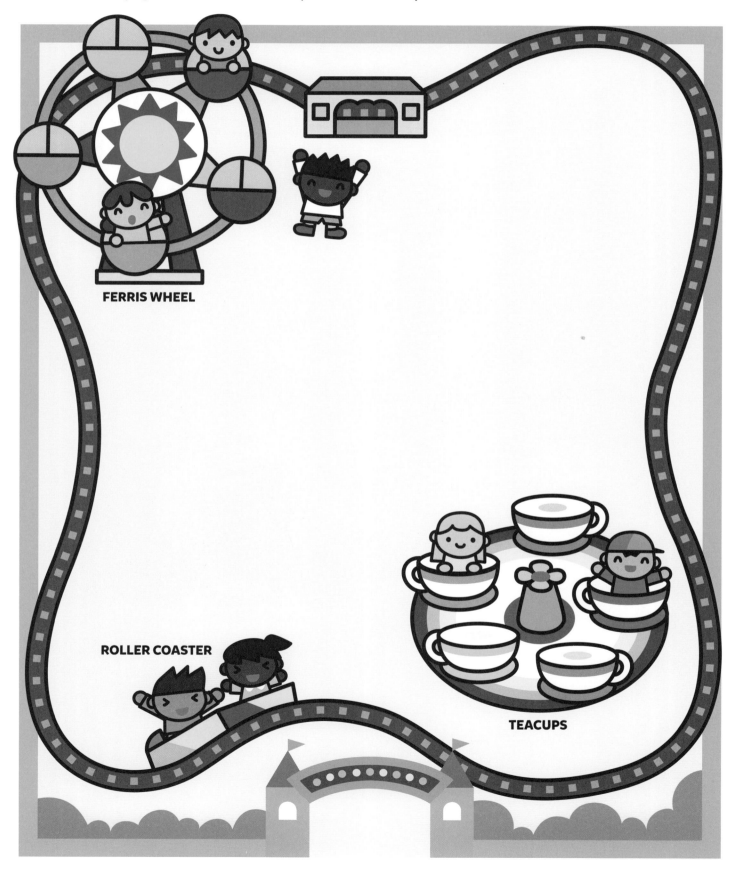

FERRIS WHEEL

ROLLER COASTER

TEACUPS

Let's Use Animal Stickers

To Parents: After your child applies the stickers, ask, "What kind of animal is in the house with the blue roof?" and "What kind of animal is in the house with the red chimney?"

Sticker

Put an animal sticker inside each house.

Let's Figure Out What's Hatching

To Parents: Help your child fold the paper. Before she or he unfolds the sheet, ask, "What kind of animal is hatching from the egg?"

Pull the bottom of the page to see what will hatch from the egg.
When you find out, say it out loud.

How to Play

First, fold the page.
Then, pull it down.

What will be born?

A chick.

Fold down

Fold up

Parents: Cut this line for your child.

Let's Figure Out What's Hiding

To Parents: Before your child unfolds the sheet, ask, "What kind of animal is hiding under the lily pad?"

Pull the bottom of the page to see what animal is hiding.
When you find out, say it out loud.

How to Play

First, fold the page.
Then, pull it down.

What is hiding?

A frog.

Fold up

Fold down

Let's Name Our Body Parts

To Parents: First, ask your child to point to each picture on the page and name each body part. Then, have your child point to and say the name of each body part on his or her body.

Where are these parts on your face? Point to each, and say it out loud.

Let's Name Our Body Parts

To Parents: First, ask your child to point to and name all of the body parts in the circles. Then, have your child point to and say the name of each body part on his or her body.

Where are these parts on your body? Point to each and say it out loud.

Let's Draw Horizontal Lines

To Parents: Have your child use a thick crayon or marker to draw the lines below. Some children may not stay inside the white area, and that is okay. With practice, their drawing will improve.

GOOD JOB!

Sticker

Draw lines from ➡ to ➡ to make the vehicles go.

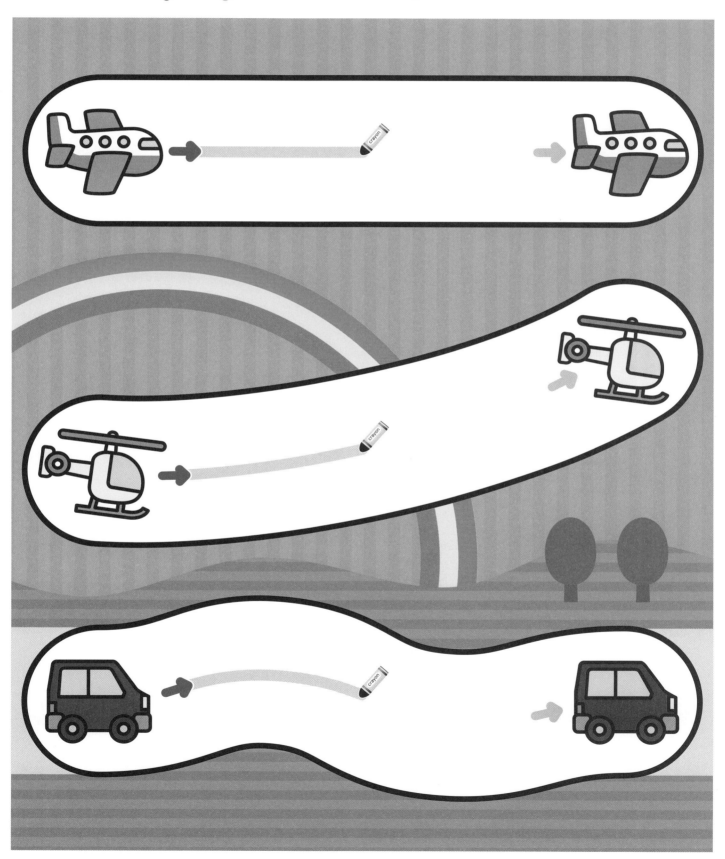

Let's Draw Bent Lines

To Parents: Have your child use a thick crayon or marker to draw lines connecting the insects. Encourage your child to stop at each bend to change direction.

Draw lines from ➡ to ➡ to make the bugs go.

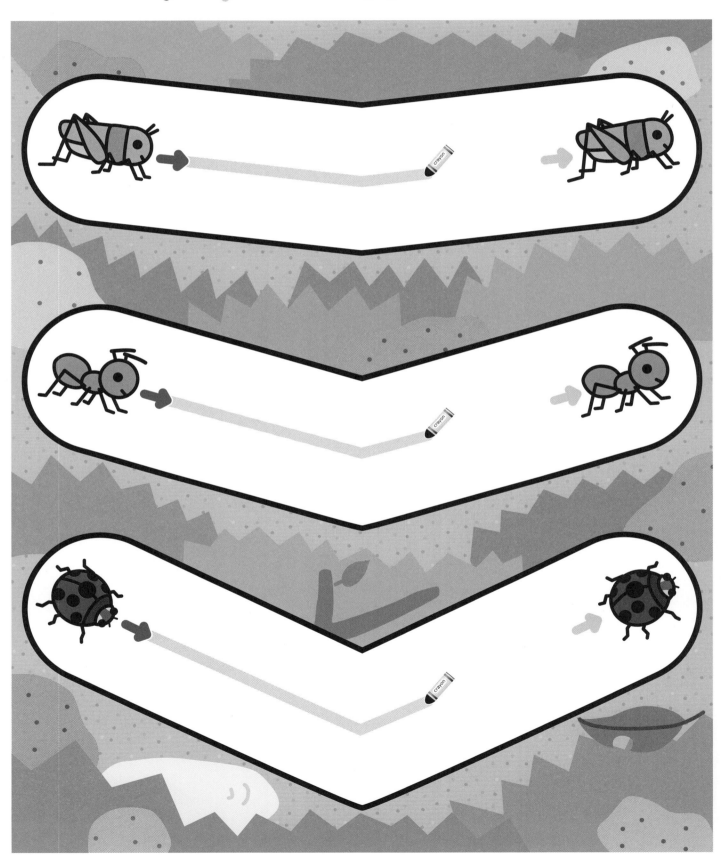

Let's Draw a Continuous Line

23

To Parents: Have your child outline the bunny by drawing a continuous line around it. It is difficult for young children to draw continuous lines. It is more important that your child have fun drawing than it is for her or him to complete the task perfectly.

GOOD JOB!
Sticker

Draw a line from to ➡ around the bunny.

Let's Draw a Continuous Line

To Parents: Have your child outline the bus by drawing one continuous line. The line should be drawn in the opposite direction from the one on the previous page. It is important for your child to learn how to draw in both directions.

GOOD JOB!

Sticker

Draw a line from ➡ to ➡ around the bus.

Let's Color the Elephant

To Parents: Have your child choose any color for the elephant. It is more important for your child to have fun coloring than it is for him or her to stay inside the lines.

Color the elephant any color you like.

Let's Color the Truck and the Bus

To Parents: Coloring builds fine motor skills and exercises creativity. It is more important for your child to have fun coloring than it is for her or him to stay inside the lines.

Color the fire truck and the bus any colors you like.

Let's Play with Food Stickers

To Parents: After your child places the stickers, say, "That sure looks good," or "Which food should we eat first?"

Put the  stickers on the plate.

Let's Draw Spaghetti

To Parents: Coloring builds fine motor skills and exercises creativity. Make sure your child draws freely, but encourage him or her to keep the spaghetti on the plate.

Draw spaghetti on the plate.

Example

Let's Get Ready to Eat

To Parents: Ask your child what he or she always does before meals (for example: wash hands). After your child tells you what he or she does, step-by-step, unfold the page and pretend to eat. Ask, "What is for lunch today?"

29

GOOD JOB!

Sticker

Push and pull the bottom of the page to make the boy eat.

How to Play

First, fold the page. Then, pull it down.

Fold up

Fold down

Parents: Cut this line for your child.

Let's Practice Our Manners

To Parents: After your child has said, "Thank you" or "May I be excused," give praise. Say, "Thank you for being polite!"

What do you say after you finish eating? Say it out loud.

Let's Get Dressed

To Parents: Using the clothing stickers at the front of the book, have your child help the boy and girl get dressed to go out and play.

Sticker

These children just finished taking a bath.
Let's help them get dressed. Put the clothing stickers on them.

Let's Put on Shoes

To Parents: Ask your child what he or she does to get ready to go outside. Then, have him or her put shoe stickers on the boy and girl.

These children want to go outside to play.
Help them get ready. Put the shoe stickers on their feet.

Let's Get Ready for Bed

To Parents: Ask your child what kinds of things she or he does to get ready for bed (for example: take a bath, put on pajamas, brush teeth, etc.) After your child has offered suggestions, have him or her help you fold the page below.

GOOD JOB!

Sticker

Let's put blankets on both of the children. Let's say, "Good night."

How to Play

Fold the page to cover the children. Pull down on the bottom of the page to uncover them.

Fold up

Fold down

Parents: Cut this line for your child.

Let's Take a Bath

To Parents: Have your child use a thick crayon or marker to draw bubbles on the page. Ask, "What do you like most about bubbles?"

GOOD JOB!
Sticker

Washing your hair is fun. Draw bubbles anywhere in this picture.

Let's Find Out Whose Hand Is Bigger

To Parents: This activity fosters an understanding of size difference. Have your child put his or her hand up against yours. Ask, "Why do you think my hand is bigger than yours?"

Put your hand on Bear's hand. Which one is bigger?

Let's Find Out Whose Foot Is Bigger

To Parents: After doing the activity below, ask your child to describe the color and shape of the penguin's foot.

Put your foot on Penguin's foot. Which one is bigger?

Let's Find Out Who Is Bigger

To Parents: Ask your child to point to the mother elephant. Ask your child why he or she chose that one. Repeat the questions for the baby elephant.

Which elephant is bigger? Make a circle around it with your finger.

MOTHER

BABY

Let's Find Out Which Is Longer

Which pants are longer? Make a circle around them with your finger.

BOY'S PANTS

MOM'S PANTS

Let's Find Out Whose Ears These Are

To Parents: Point to each animal along the bottom of the page. Ask your child to name each animal as you point to it. Have your child make a line from the ears to the matching animal with his or her finger before using a crayon.

Which ears belong to which animal?
Draw a line between the matching ears and faces.

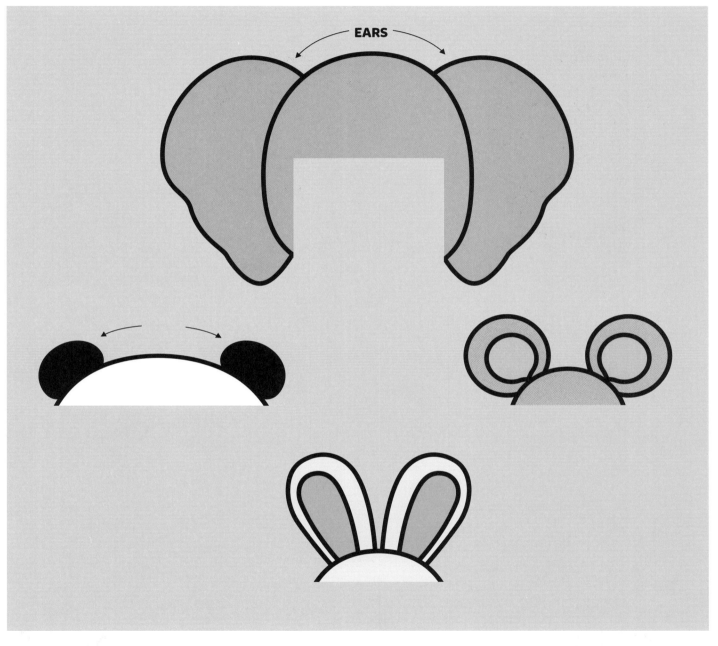

EARS

ELEPHANT   **PANDA**   **MOUSE**   **RABBIT**

Let's Find Out Whose Tails These Are

Which tail belongs to which animal?
Draw a line between the matching tails and faces.

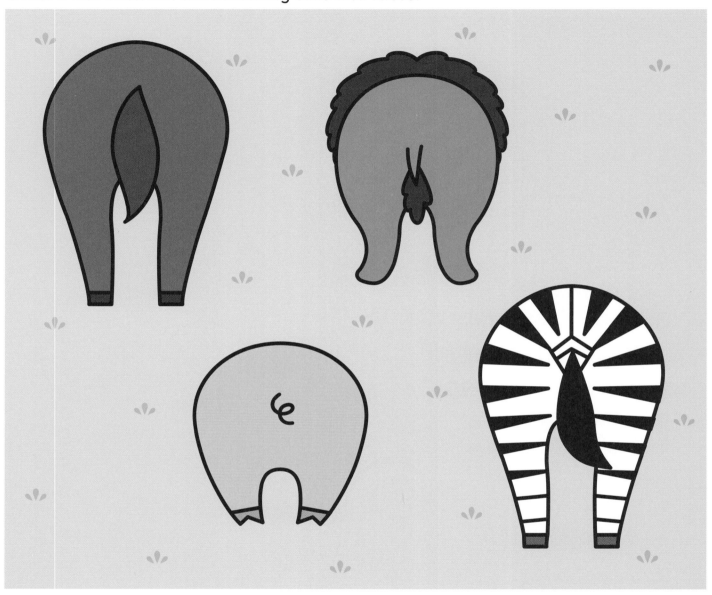

LION **ZEBRA** **PIG** **HORSE**

Let's Find Out Where the Object Is

To Parents: Cut out the acorn, strawberry, and candy for your child. Next, place the strawberry in one of the bear's paws. Fold the page so the strawberry is hidden. Ask, "Which paw is the strawberry in?" Repeat with the acorn and candy.

Which paw is holding the strawberry? Point with your finger.
Pull down the flap to find out.

How to Play

Place an object in the bear's paw and fold the page up to hide it.

Fold up

Let's Imitate Animals

To Parents: Encourage your child to use his or her entire body as well as his or her voice to imitate different animals and their behaviors. Start with a rabbit and an elephant, then pretend to be a dog, a cat, a mouse, and other animals.

GOOD JOB!

Sticker

Let's pretend to be a rabbit.

Let's pretend to be an elephant.

I can hop like a rabbit.

I can swing my arm like an elephant swings its trunk.

I can walk like an elephant, too.

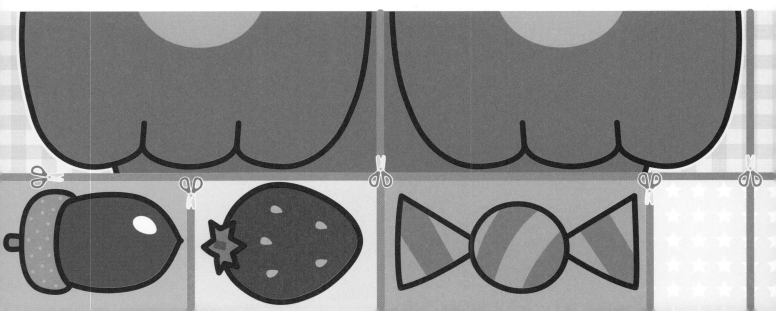

Let's Use Fruit Stickers

To Parents: Use the fruit stickers from the front of the book. When your child is done, say, "That looks delicious," and pretend to eat the sundae.

Put the  stickers on the ice cream sundae.

Let's Make a Kid's Meal

To Parents: Use the stickers from the front of the book. Say, "Today you are the cook. Why don't you make lunch?"

Sticker

Let's make lunch. Put the stickers on the plate.

Let's Make Shapes

To Parents: Have your child use a thick crayon or marker to trace the square. Have him or her say its name out loud while tracing. Then, trace the shape with your finger, and say, "This is a square. What other things are shaped like a square?"

Let's trace the square.

Let's Make Shapes

To Parents: Have your child use a thick crayon or marker to trace the circle. Have him or her say its name out loud while tracing. Then, trace the shape with your finger, and say, "This is a circle. What other things are shaped like a circle?"

Let's trace the circle.

Let's Make Shapes

To Parents: Have your child use a thick crayon or marker to trace the triangle. Have him or her say its name out loud while tracing. Then, trace the shape with your finger, and say, "This is a triangle. What other things are shaped like a triangle?"

Let's trace the triangle.

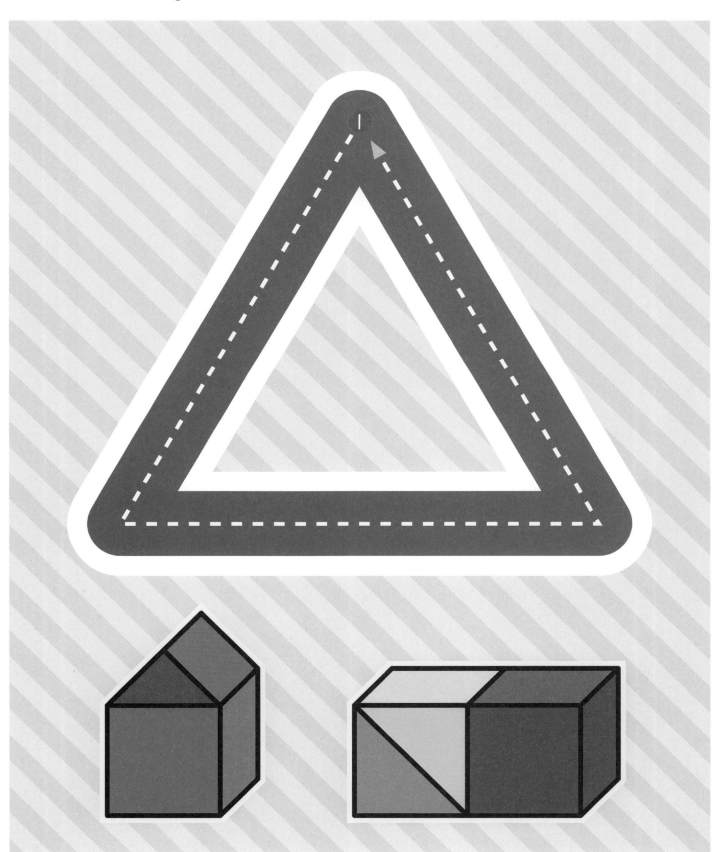

Let's Make Shapes

To Parents: Have your child use a thick crayon or marker to trace the rectangle. Have him or her say its name out loud while tracing. Then, trace the shape with your finger, and say, "This is a rectangle. What other things are shaped like a rectangle?"

GOOD JOB!

Sticker

Let's trace the rectangle.

Let's Name the Vehicles

To Parents: Point to each vehicle and ask your child to tell you its name. If your child doesn't know the name (train, bus, boat, fire engine, police car, airplane), tell him or her.

GOOD JOB!

Sticker

What kinds of vehicles are these? Say their names out loud.

Let's Name the Dishes and Utensils

To Parents: Extend the activity by asking more questions. "Which utensil has a blue handle?" "What is the biggest item on the page?"

GOOD JOB!

Sticker

What do you see in this picture?
Say the names of the items out loud.

Let's Name the Food

To Parents: Make the activity more fun by talking about the foods on the page. Ask, "Which ones are your favorites?" Pretend to share and eat the dishes.

GOOD JOB!

Sticker

What kinds of foods are these? Say their names out loud.

Let's Name the Food

GOOD JOB!

Sticker

What kinds of foods are these? Say their names out loud.

Let's Draw Eyes and a Mouth

To Parents: Ask your child to draw one sad, one angry, and one happy face. Encourage your child to draw an original face and not just copy the example.

Make the houses into faces. Draw eyes in the windows. Draw a mouth in each door.

Example

Let's Draw a Face

To Parents: Encourage your child to draw an original face and not just copy the example.

Let's draw a face on each flower.

Example

Let's Decide Which Road to Take

To Parents: Prior to the activity, cut out the train (for the next page) and the puppy. Then, help your child fold and glue the puppy game piece together.

Move the puppy from ➡ to ➡ to help it get to its mother.

How to Make the Game Piece

Fold and glue it.

Use on page 56.

Use on this page.

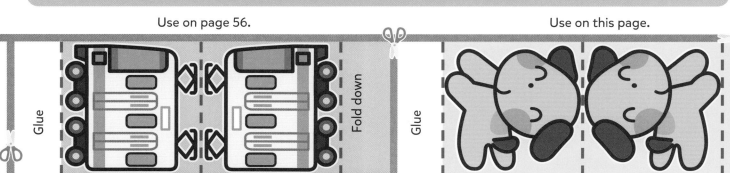

Glue · Fold down · Glue · Fold down

Let's Decide Which Track to Take

To Parents: Prior to the activity, cut out the train picture (located on the previous page). Then, help your child fold and glue the game piece together.

GOOD JOB!

Sticker

Move the game piece from ➡ to ➡ to help the train get to the station.

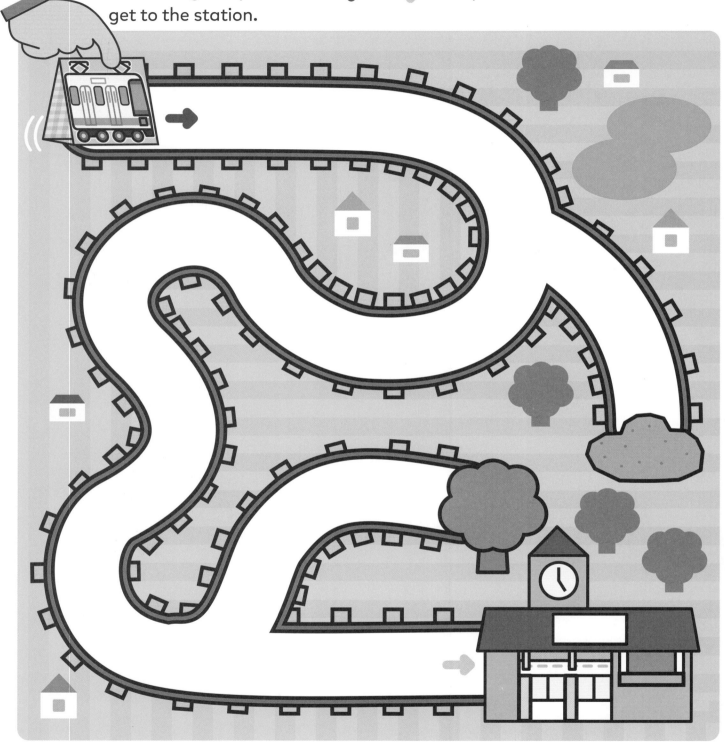

Use on page 55.

Use on this page.

Let's Decide Which Way to Go

To Parents: First, have your child use his or her finger to trace a path through the cat. Then, have your child use a crayon.

Draw a path from ➡ to ➡ through the cat's body.

Let's Decide Which Way to Go

To Parents: Have your child use a crayon to draw a path through the dog. If your child is not ready for that, he or she may use a finger to trace the path.

Draw a path from ➡ to ➡ through the dog's body.

Let's Match the Cups

To Parents: To help, ask your child to point to the two red cups that match, the two yellow cups that match, and so on. For an added challenge, have your child name the color of each cup.

GOOD JOB!

Sticker

Which cups match? Point with your finger.

Let's Match the Trains

To Parents: If your child does not recognize the pairs right away, call attention to the details, such as the shapes or colors of the trains.

Which trains match? Draw a line to connect each match.

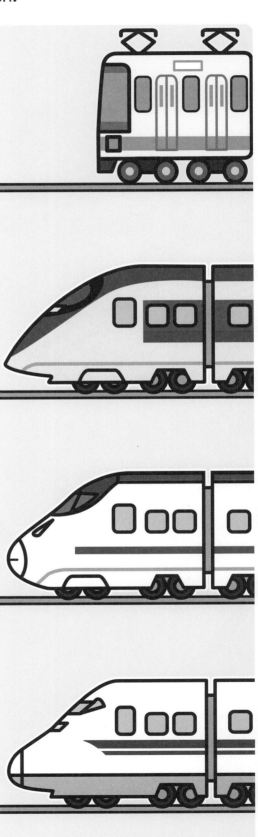

Let's Match the Animals

To Parents: When your child makes a match, have him or her say the animal's name out loud (bird, turtle, rabbit, lion, monkey). Then, go over the rest of the animals on the page together.

GOOD JOB!

Sticker

Point to the animals in the picture that match the ones in the example box.

Example

Let's Match the Playground Objects

To Parents: When your child makes a match, have him or her say the name of the item out loud (bucket, girl, tricycle, car). Go over the rest of the items together.

Circle the objects in the picture that match the ones in the example box.

Let's Color the Pasta

To Parents: Have your child use thick crayons or markers to add whatever she or he wants to the noodles on the plate. Encourage your child to use different colors for different objects.

Let's add meatballs or vegetables to the pasta.
Use as many colors as you want.

Let's Color

To Parents: Have your child use thick crayons or markers to color the ice cream scoops. After your child finishes coloring, ask, "What ice cream flavors did you make?"

Let's color the ice cream scoops. Use as many colors as you want.